THiS BOOK BELONGS TO:

Thomas

Clefairy

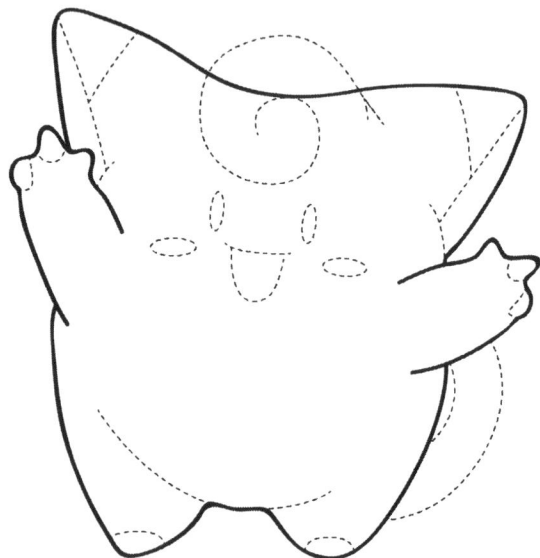

Practice Page

Clefairy

Weedle

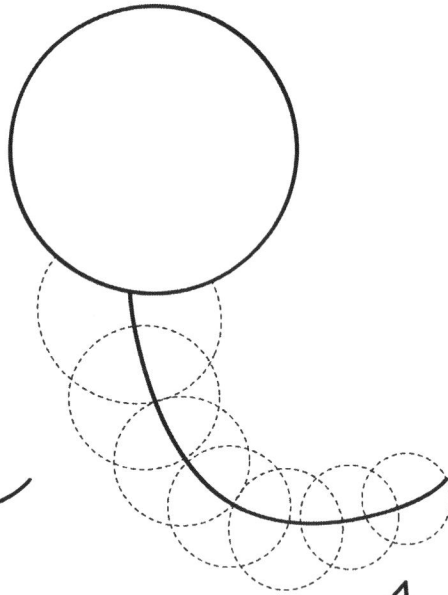

Practice Page

Practice Page

Weedle

Pidgey

Practice Page

Pidgey

Butterfree

Practice Page

Butterfree

Raticate

Practice Page

Raticate

Arbok

Practice Page

Arbok

Zubat

Practice Page

Zubat

Meowth

Practice Page

Practice Page

Meowth

Parasect

Practice Page

Parasect

Weepinbell

Practice Page

Practice Page

Weepinbell

Pikachu

Practice Page

Practice Page

Pikachu

Wartortle

Practice Page

Practice Page

Wartortle

Oddish

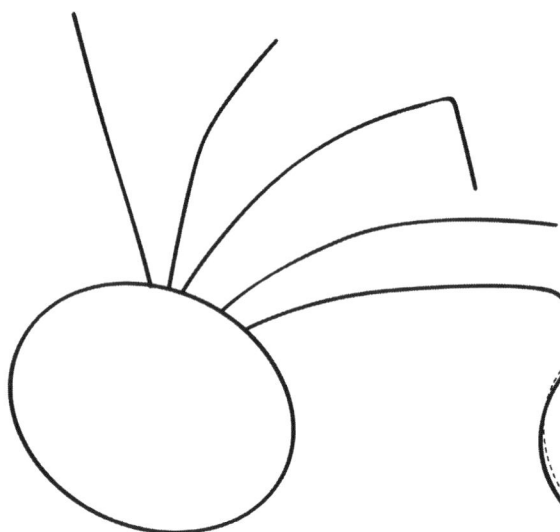

Practice Page

Oddish

Vulpix

Vulpix

Charmander

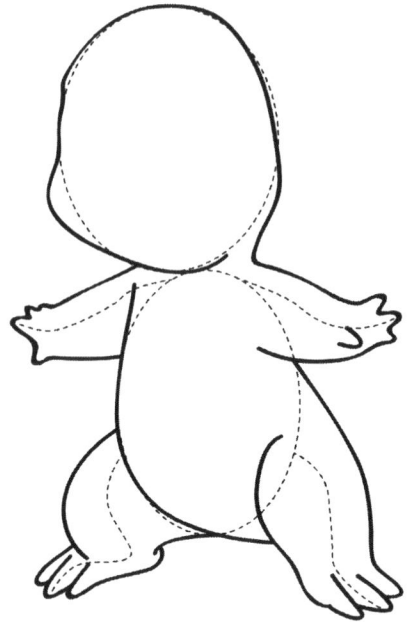

Practice Page

Practice Page

Charmander

Ponyta

Practice Page

Ponyta

Mankey

Practice Page

Practice Page

Mankey

Diglett

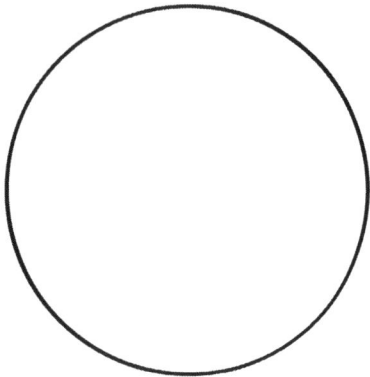

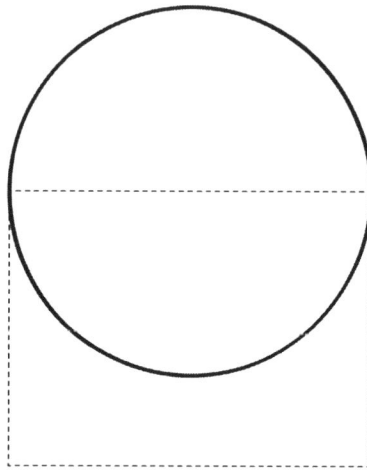

Practice Page

Diglett

Ivysaur

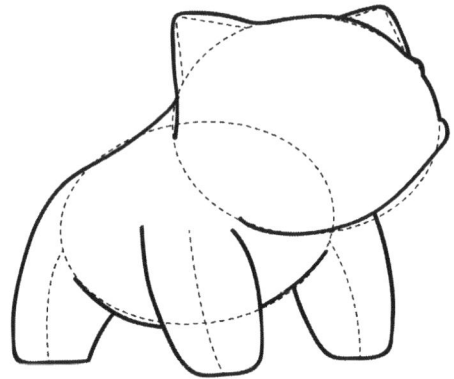

Practice Page

Ivysaur

Caterpie

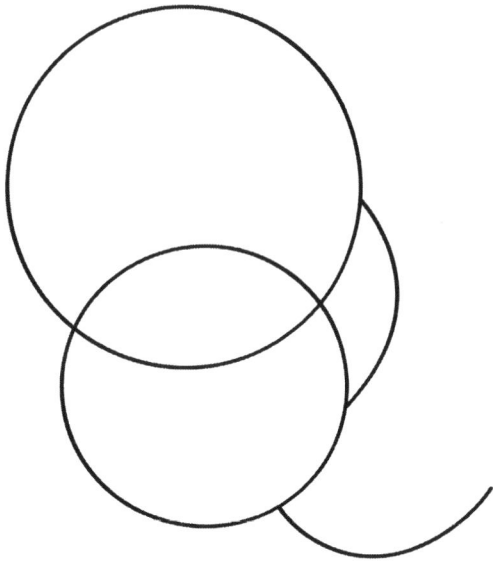

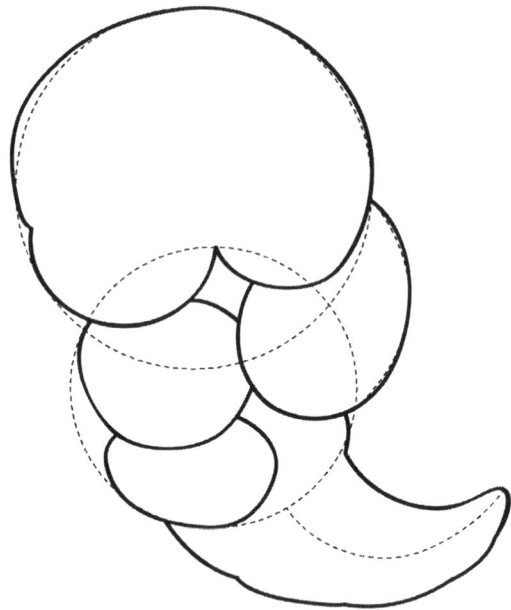

Practice Page

Caterpie

Psyduck

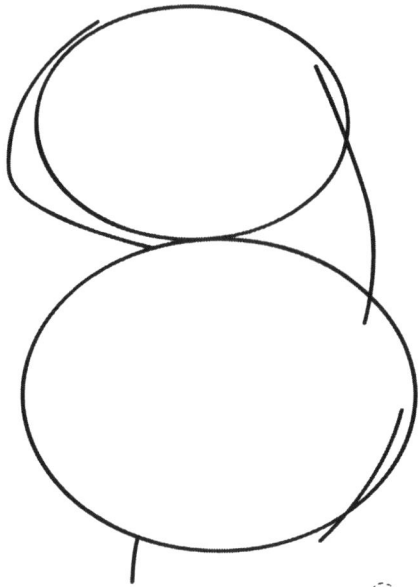

Practice Page

Psyduck

Slowpoke

Practice Page

Slowpoke

Doduo

Practice Page

Doduo

Seel

Practice Page

Seel

Poliwhirl

Practice Page

Poliwhirl

Printed in Great Britain
by Amazon